Who... ? At school

Vic Parker

Heinemann LIBRARY

Little Nippers

www.heinemann.co.uk/library

Visit our website to find out more information about **Heinemann Library** books.

To order:
- ☎ Phone 44 (0) 1865 888066
- 🖹 Send a fax to 44 (0) 1865 314091
- 💻 Visit the Heinemann Bookshop at www.heinemann.co.uk/library to browse our catalogue and order online.

First published in Great Britain by Heinemann Library, Halley Court, Jordan Hill, Oxford OX2 8EJ, part of Harcourt Education. Heinemann is a registered trademark of Harcourt Education Ltd.

Editorial: Jilly Attwood and Claire Throp
Design: Jo Hinton-Malivoire and bigtop, Bicester, UK
Models made by: Jo Brooker
Picture Research: Rosie Garai
Production: Séverine Ribierre

Originated by Dot Gradations
Printed and bound in China by South China Printing Company

ISBN 0 431 17321 4 (hardback)
08 07 06 05 04
10 9 8 7 6 5 4 3 2 1

ISBN 0 431 17326 5 (paperback)
08 07 06 05 04
10 9 8 7 6 5 4 3 2 1

British Library Cataloguing in Publication Data
Parker, Vic
At school – (Who helps us?)
372
A full catalogue record for this book is available from the British Library.

Acknowledgements
The publishers would like to thank the following for permission to reproduce photographs:
Peter Evans Photography pp. **4**, **5**, **6–7**, **8–9**, **10**, **11**, **14–15**, **16–17**, **18**, **19**, **22**, **23**; Sally and Richard Greenhill pp. **12–13**, **20–21**.

Cover photograph reproduced with permission of Peter Evans Photography.

The publishers would like to thank Annie Davy for her assistance in the preparation of this book.

Every effort has been made to contact copyright holders of any material reproduced in this book. Any omissions will be rectified in subsequent printings if notice is given to the publishers.

Contents

Early morning at school

Who is the first person to arrive at school every day?

It is the caretaker, with a big bunch of keys.

Going to school

crossing patrol assistant

Who helps you to cross the road safely?

7

School begins

Llyfrau
Mawr

The teacher takes the register to check everyone is here.

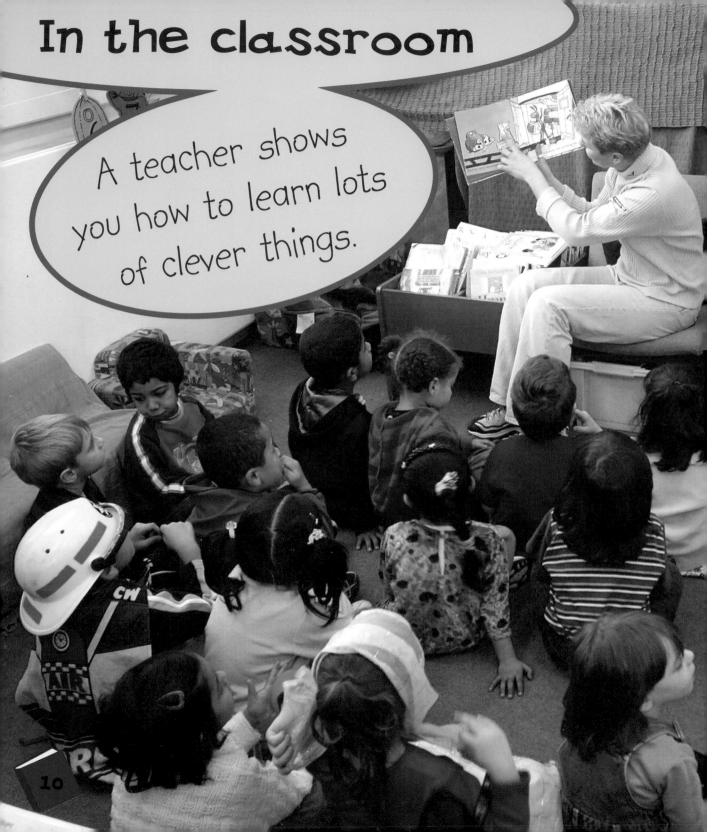

In the classroom

A teacher shows you how to learn lots of clever things.

A classroom assistant
gives you extra help.

Going on a trip

Who takes you on a day out?

Feeling hungry

lunchtime assistant

Do you know who helps us?

Yum-yum!

It's lunchtime.

The secretary works in the office.

In the library

There are lots of lovely books in the library.

The person who helps you choose
one is called the librarian.

19

Fun after school

School is over. It's time for club.

A dance teacher gets everyone **moving** and **grooving!**

Home time!

See you tomorrow.

Bye-bye!

Index

The end

Notes for adults

The *Who helps us . . .?* series looks at a variety of people that a young child may come across in different situations. The books explore who these people are, why we might interact with them, and how to communicate appropriately. Used together, the books will enable discussion about similarities and differences between environments and people, and encourage the growth of the child's sense of self. The following Early Learning Goals are relevant to this series:

Knowledge and understanding of the world
Early learning goals for a sense of place:
• show an interest in the world in which they live
• notice differences between features of the local environment
• observe, find out about and identify features in the place they live and the natural world
• find out about their environment, and talk about those features they like and dislike.

Personal, social and emotional development
Early learning goals for a sense of community:
• make connections between different parts of their life experience
• understand that people have different needs, views, cultures and beliefs, which need to be treated with respect.

Early learning goals for self-confidence and self-esteem:
• separate from main carer with support/confidence
• express needs and feelings in appropriate ways
• initiate interactions with other people
• have a sense of self as a member of different communities
• respond to significant experiences, showing a range of feelings when appropriate
• have a developing awareness of their own needs, views and feelings and be sensitive to the needs, views and feelings of others.

This book introduces the reader to a range of people they may come across when at school. It will encourage young children to think about the jobs these people perform and how they help the community. **At school** will help children extend their vocabulary, as they will hear new words such as *caretaker* and *register*. You may like to introduce and explain other new words yourself, such as *lunch break* and *first aid kit*.

Follow-up activities
• Role play a lesson at school, with the child as the teacher and the grown-up as the pupil.
• Cross a road with the help of a crossing patrol assistant, practising the green cross code.
• Draw and cut out some pictures of food. Ask two or three of the children to play at serving school lunches to the other children.